◆ LET'S EXPLORE SCIENCE ◐

Water & Floating

▲ David Evans and Claudette Williams ▢

DORLING KINDERSLEY
London ▪ New York ▪ Stuttgart

A DORLING KINDERSLEY BOOK

Project Editor Dawn Sirett
Art Editor Karen Fielding
Managing Editor Jane Yorke
Managing Art Editor Chris Scollen
Production Jayne Wood
Photography by Susanna Price

First published in Great Britain in 1993
by Dorling Kindersley Limited,
9 Henrietta Street, London WC2E 8PS

A CIP catalogue record for this book is
available from the British Library.

ISBN 0-7513-5018-4

Reproduced by J. Film Process Singapore Pte., Ltd.
Printed and bound in Belgium by Proost

Dorling Kindersley would like to thank the following for their help
in producing this book: Daniel Pangbourne and Dave King (for
additional photography); Coral Mula (for safety symbol artwork);
Mark Richards (for jacket design); Julia Fletcher; and the Franklin
Delano Roosevelt School, London. Dorling Kindersley would
also like to give special thanks to the following for appearing
in this book: Natalie Agada; Sammy Arias; Hannah Capleton;
Sapphire Elia; Foyzul Kadir; Tony Locke; Gemma Loke;
Rachael Malicki; Paul Miller; Kim Ng; Maxwell Ralph;
Daniel Sach; Anthony Singh; Ahmani Vidal-Simon;
and George Woolgrove.

Contents

Note to parents and teachers

Young children are forever asking questions about the things they see, touch, hear, smell, and taste. The **Let's Explore Science** series aims to foster children's natural curiosity and encourages them to use their senses to find out about science. Each book features a variety of experiments based on one topic, which draw on a young child's everyday experiences. By investigating familiar activities, such as bouncing a ball, making cakes, or clapping hands, young children will learn that science plays an important part in the world around them.

Investigative approach

Young children can only begin to understand science if they are stimulated to think and to find out for themselves. For these reasons, an open-ended questioning approach is used in the **Let's Explore Science** books and, wherever possible, results of experiments are not shown. Children are encouraged to make their own scientific discoveries and to interpret them according to their own ideas. This investigative approach to learning makes science exciting and not just about acquiring "facts". This way of learning will assist children in many areas of their education.

Using the books

Before starting an experiment, check the text and pictures to ensure that you have assembled any necessary equipment. Allow children to help in this process and to suggest materials to use. Once ready, it is important to let children decide how to carry out the experiment and what the result means to them. You can help by asking questions, such as "What do you think will happen?" or "What did you do?"

Household equipment

All the experiments can be carried out easily at home. In most cases, inexpensive household objects and materials are used.

Guide to experiments

The *Guide to experiments* on pages 28-29 is intended to help parents, teachers, or helpers using this book with children. It gives an outline of the scientific principles underlying the experiments, includes useful tips for carrying out the activities, suggests alternative equipment to use, and additional activities to try.

Safe experimenting

This symbol appears next to experiments where children may require adult supervision or assistance, for example, when they are heating things or using sharp tools.

About this book

Water and Floating enables children to investigate the nature of water and other liquids. The experiments demonstrate that water can exist in different states, i.e., solid (ice), liquid (water), or gas (steam), and that each of these states has different properties. Children will find out that:

- some liquids mix with water and some solids dissolve in water;

- liquids can flow, fill the shape of a container, form drops, and make surfaces wet;

- liquids will find their own level when left;

- liquids exert upward forces that prevent objects from sinking unless those objects can exert greater forces downwards;

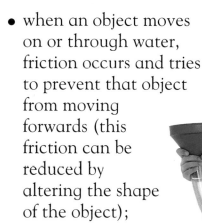

- when an object moves on or through water, friction occurs and tries to prevent that object from moving forwards (this friction can be reduced by altering the shape of the object);

- dirty water can be made clean and that plants and animals need clean water if they are to stay healthy.

With your help, young children will enjoy exploring the world of science and discover that finding out is fun.

David Evans and Claudette Williams

What is water like?

What does water taste, smell, feel, and sound like?

Looking and smelling
What does water look like? What does water smell like?

Looking at water level
Hold a bottle of water at different angles. Does the level of the water stay the same?

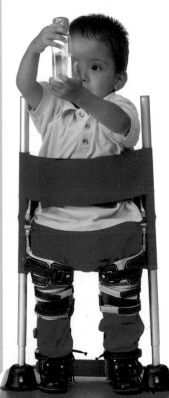

fizzy mineral water

tap water

Tasting
Does mineral water taste the same as tap water? What does water taste like when you add salt to it?

still mineral water

salty water

10

Listening to water
Does water make a sound when you pour it?

Does water make a different sound when you shake it in a bottle?

Adding bath salts
What does water feel like when you add bath salts to it?

Feeling water
What does water feel like?

Wearing gloves
What does water feel like if you wear woollen gloves or rubber gloves?

Take care in a paddling pool.

11

Will it mix with water?

What things will mix with water?
What will mix with other liquids?

Do not taste the liquids.

Liquids
What different liquids can you find?

vegetable oil

vinegar

syrup

perfume

water

washing-up liquid

Is water a liquid? Is syrup a liquid? Is vegetable oil a liquid?

Do all liquids smell the same? Do all liquids pour?

Mixtures

Try adding some of the things on this page to water. What do you see? Which ones dissolve? What will happen if you stir the mixtures with a spoon or a hand whisk?

Drops

What happens when you add a drop of food colouring to water?

vegetable oil and bath salts

rice

baking powder

vinegar

water

flour

milk

butter

brown sugar

bath salts

Shake some vegetable oil and bath salts in a jar for a long time. What happens?

What happens when you add baking powder to vinegar?

13

Is water always a liquid?

Try these experiments to find out
if water is always a liquid.

Cold water

What will happen if
you leave water in a
freezer overnight?

Cold bottle

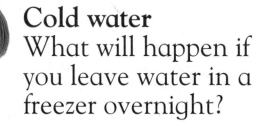 Leave
a bottle
in a fridge for
an hour. What
happens to the
bottle when
you take it
out of the
fridge?

Cold mirror

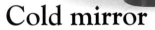 Put a hand mirror in the fridge. Leave
it for an hour. What happens when
you hold the cold mirror over a warm drink?

Water and ice

Leave some water in a warm place for a long time. What happens? What happens when you leave ice-cubes out of the freezer?

Ice

What do you think will happen if you leave ice in water for a long time?

How warm is ice? How warm is water from the tap? Can you use a thermometer to find out? Ask an adult to help you.

Fruit and vegetables

Can you make a liquid by squeezing fruit or vegetables? Is it water?

What shape is water?

Can you change the shape of water?

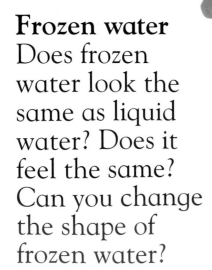

Water in a bag
 Ask an adult to help you to fill a plastic bag with water. How can you change its shape?

Frozen water
Does frozen water look the same as liquid water? Does it feel the same? Can you change the shape of frozen water?

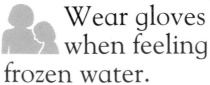 Wear gloves when feeling frozen water.

Drip race
Put drops of water, washing-up liquid, or vegetable oil on a mirror.

Which liquid will run down the mirror the fastest?

Drops of water

Can you make drops of water hang from your fingers? What shape are the drops?

Will the shape of the drops be the same when you drip them on to different materials?

grease-proof paper

plastic

velvet

kitchen foil

dropper

toilet paper

Put a drop of water on different kinds of paper using a dropper. What happens? Which paper would be the best for mopping up a spilt drink?

tissue

tissue paper

kitchen towel

Can you fill it with water?

How quickly can you fill and empty different things?

Filling bottles

Put some empty plastic bottles into water. Which one fills up the fastest?

Filling with a jug

Can you use a jug of water to fill some bottles? Is it easier to fill the bottles if you use a funnel?

Emptying a jug

How many cups can you fill with one jug of water?

Filling cups

Try putting plastic cups into water at different angles. Do they always fill with water?

Put a plastic cup under water. Turn the cup upside-down and slowly lift it out of the tank. What happens?

Emptying bottles

 Ask an adult to help you to make some holes like these in plastic bottles.

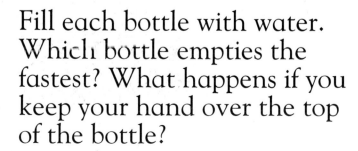

Fill each bottle with water. Which bottle empties the fastest? What happens if you keep your hand over the top of the bottle?

Can you move water?

Can you move water from one place to another?

With a straw
Can you move water using a drinking straw?

With a spoon
Can you move water using a spoon? What happens if you use a sieve?

With your hands
Can you move water using one hand? Is it easier with two hands?

What other things can you find that will move water?

With a tube
Fill a tube with water. Use a funnel to help you.

What happens if you lift one end of the tube?

With bottles
Can you move water using a squeezy bottle or a spray bottle?

With a siphon
Hold a tube under water so that it fills up with water. Leave one end of the tube in the water. Put your hand over the other end and lift it out of the water.

What happens when you hold this end of the tube over a lower bowl and take your hand away?

What happens if the two bowls are at the same level?

21

Will it float on water?

Find some different things to drop into water. Can you guess which ones will float?

Floating things
What will happen when you drop your things into water? Will they float or will they sink?

Drop a hard-boiled egg and an uncooked egg into the water. What happens?

Ice
Do you think ice will float in these different liquids?

water

salty water

syrup

vegetable oil

Table-tennis ball
Hold a table-tennis ball under water. What does it feel like? What happens when you let go of the ball?

Plastic bowl
How many ways can you find to make a plastic bowl sink?

Modelling clay
Can you make a piece of modelling clay float? Can you make it sink?

Will it move in water?

Try these experiments to see if you can make things move in water.

plastic tray

plastic pot

Moving things
How can you make things move in water? What can you use?

Moving trays and pots
Find some plastic trays or pots of different shapes to use as boats.

Which tray or pot will move through the water the fastest?

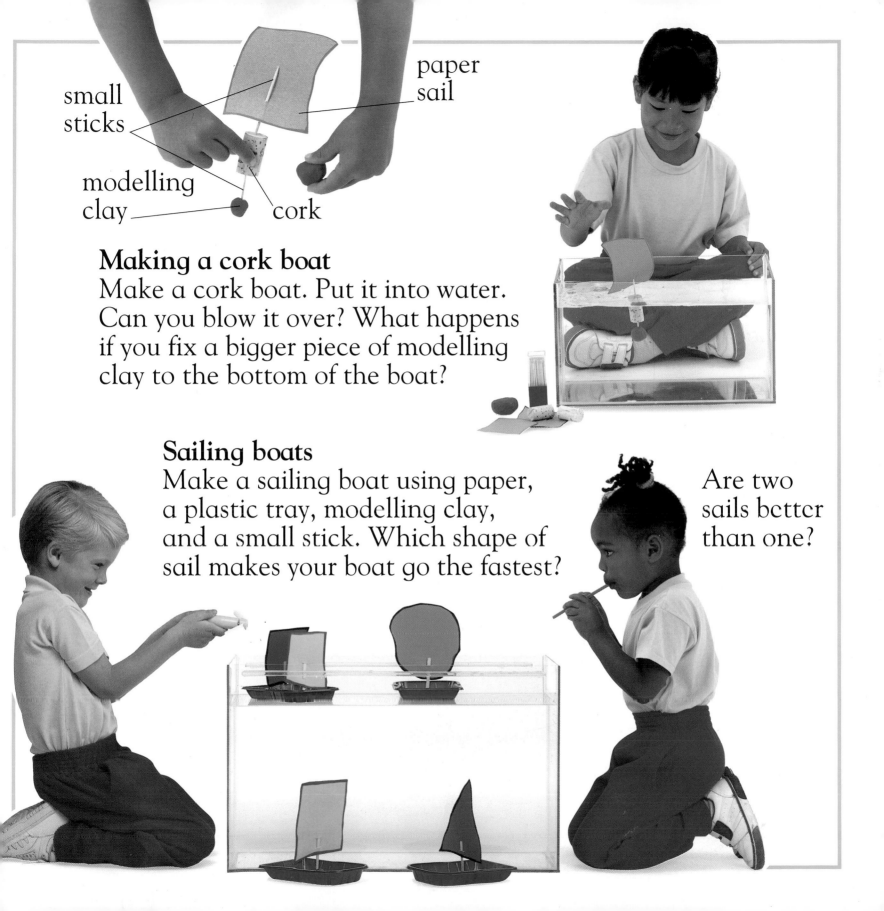

small sticks

paper sail

modelling clay

cork

Making a cork boat

Make a cork boat. Put it into water. Can you blow it over? What happens if you fix a bigger piece of modelling clay to the bottom of the boat?

Sailing boats

Make a sailing boat using paper, a plastic tray, modelling clay, and a small stick. Which shape of sail makes your boat go the fastest?

Are two sails better than one?

Can you clean water?

Can you make water dirty using some soil? Can you make it clean again?

 Wear gloves when doing these experiments and do not drink the water.

Gravel filter
Can you make a gravel filter? What happens to dirty water when you pour it into the gravel filter?

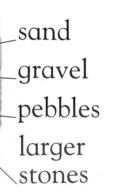

sand
gravel
pebbles
larger stones

Filters
Can you use a colander, sieve, or coffee filter-paper to clean dirty water? Which one cleans dirty water the best?

Flannel filter
Set up two bowls and a flannel like this.

flannel

empty bowl

dirty water

What happens to the dirty water? Now try using kitchen towel or cotton wool instead of a flannel.

wool

kitchen towel

muslin plastic

cotton

Different materials
Spoon some dirty water on to different materials. Which material cleans dirty water the best?

Which material would you use for a raincoat to keep you dry?

Aquarium
Can you think of some plants and animals that need clean water to live in?

When do you use clean water?

Index

Guide to experiments

The notes below briefly outline the scientific principles underlying the experiments and include suggestions for alternative equipment to use and activities to try.

What is water like? 10-11

Using their senses of touch, taste, smell, sight, and hearing, children explore the properties of water. They find that water is a colourless liquid that does not have a strong taste or smell.

Will it mix with water? 12-13

Here children start by comparing the properties of various liquids. By pouring the liquids, children discover that liquids flow at different rates. Children could also be asked to look at the way salt or flour flows and to decide if these substances are liquids. Adding a range of solids and other liquids to water helps children to understand that some solids dissolve in water and some liquids mix with water.

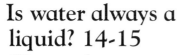

Is water always a liquid? 14-15

Water is shown to change from a liquid to a solid, or from a gas to a liquid. Water vapour in the air condenses into water on the cold bottle and mirror. Children could also watch an adult hold a metal spoon in the steam from a boiling kettle and observe the steam condensing into liquid water on the cold spoon. When children leave water in a warm place, it evaporates. By squeezing liquids from fruit or vegetables, children can begin to appreciate that living things contain large amounts of water.

What shape is water? 16-17

Here children discover that liquid water flows and spreads, but ice doesn't. They also examine water drops and find that they "cling" to some materials, but are absorbed by others.

Can you fill it with water? 18-19

Children learn about capacity by filling and emptying containers. When emptying bottles with holes in them, children will find that the more water there is above the holes, the greater the pressure forcing the water out of the holes.

Can you move water? 20-21

Children have found that water can flow and be squirted under pressure. They now use this knowledge to help them to find ways of moving water. When making a siphon, children can find it difficult to remove the air from the tube. Under supervision, they should try sucking the end of the tube until water flows.

Will it float on water? 22-23

Children find that liquids exert an upward force on an object. This force prevents an object from sinking unless that object can exert a greater force downwards. When holding a table-tennis ball under water, children will feel an upward force trying to make the ball float. Modelling clay floats if it is shaped like a boat.

Will it move in water? 24-25

By floating the trays and pots, children form ideas about the ideal shape for an object if it is to overcome friction when moving through water. In the cork boat activity, using a larger piece of clay makes the boat more stable. Finally, by keeping the same boat hull and changing the sail, children find the best type of sail for their boat.

Can you clean water? 26-27

Children use various filters to clean muddy water. As the filtered water could still contain harmful microbes, make sure that children do not drink it. By looking at an aquarium, children begin to see the need for clean water to support plant and animal life.